IN CONGRESS, JULY

The unanimous Declaration of the thirteen united States of America.

When in the Course of human events, it becomes necessary for one people to dissolve the political bands which have connected them with another, and to assume among the powers of the earth, the separate and equal station to which the Laws of Nature and of Nature's God entitle them, a decent respect to the opinions of mankind requires that they should declare the causes which impel them to the separation.

We hold these truths to be self-evident, that all men are created equal, that they are endowed by their Creator with certain unalienable Rights, that among these are Life, Liberty and the pursuit of Happiness.—That to secure these rights, Governments are instituted among Men, deriving their just powers from the consent of the governed,—That whenever any Form of Government becomes destructive of these ends, it is the Right of the People to alter or to abolish it, and to institute new Government, laying its foundation on such principles and organizing its powers in such form, as to them shall seem most likely to effect their Safety and Happiness. Prudence, indeed, will dictate that Governments long established should not be changed for light and transient causes; and accordingly all experience hath shewn, that mankind are more disposed to suffer, while evils are sufferable, than to right themselves by abolishing the forms to which they are accustomed. But when a long train of abuses and usurpations, pursuing invariably the same Object evinces a design to reduce them under absolute Despotism, it is their right, it is their duty, to throw off such Government, and to provide new Guards for their future security.—Such has been the patient sufferance of these Colonies; and such is now the necessity which constrains them to alter their former Systems of Government. The history of the present King of Great Britain is a history of repeated injuries and usurpations, all having in direct object the establishment of an absolute Tyranny over these States. To prove this, let Facts be submitted to a candid world.

He has refused his Assent to Laws, the most wholesome and necessary for the public good.—He has forbidden his Governors to pass Laws of immediate and pressing importance, unless suspended in their operation till his Assent should be obtained; and when so suspended, he has utterly neglected to attend to them.—He has refused to pass other Laws for the accommodation of large districts of people, unless those people would relinquish the right of Representation in the Legislature, a right inestimable to them and formidable to tyrants only.—He has called together legislative bodies at places unusual, uncomfortable, and distant from the depository of their public Records, for the sole purpose of fatiguing them into compliance with his measures.—He has dissolved Representative Houses repeatedly, for opposing with manly firmness his invasions on the rights of the people.—He has refused for a long time, after such dissolutions, to cause others to be elected; whereby the Legislative powers, incapable of Annihilation, have returned to the People at large for their exercise; the State remaining in the mean time exposed to all the dangers of invasion from without, and convulsions within.—He has endeavoured to prevent the population of these States; for that purpose obstructing the Laws for Naturalization of Foreigners; refusing to pass others to encourage their migrations hither, and raising the conditions of new Appropriations of Lands.—He has obstructed the Administration of Justice, by refusing his Assent to Laws for establishing Judiciary powers.—He has made Judges dependent on his Will alone, for the tenure of their offices, and the amount and payment of their salaries.—He has erected a multitude of New Offices, and sent hither swarms of Officers to harass our people, and eat out their substance.—He has kept among us, in times of peace, Standing Armies without the Consent of our legislatures.—He has affected to render the Military independent of and superior to the Civil power.—He has combined with others to subject us to a jurisdiction foreign to our constitution, and unacknowledged by our laws; giving his Assent to their Acts of pretended Legislation:—For Quartering large bodies of armed troops among us:—For protecting them, by a mock Trial, from punishment for any Murders which they should commit on the Inhabitants of these States:—For cutting off our Trade with all parts of the world:—For imposing Taxes on us without our Consent:—For depriving us in many cases, of the benefits of Trial by Jury:—For transporting us beyond Seas to be tried for pretended offences:—For abolishing the free System of English Laws in a neighbouring Province, establishing therein an Arbitrary government, and enlarging its Boundaries so as to render it at once an example and fit instrument for introducing the same absolute rule into these Colonies:—For taking away our Charters, abolishing our most valuable Laws, and altering fundamentally the Forms of our Governments:—For suspending our own Legislatures, and declaring themselves invested with power to legislate for us in all cases whatsoever.—He has abdicated Government here, by declaring us out of his Protection and waging War against us.—He has plundered our seas, ravaged our Coasts, burnt our towns, and destroyed the lives of our people.—He is at this time transporting large Armies of foreign Mercenaries to compleat the works of death, desolation and tyranny, already begun with circumstances of Cruelty & perfidy scarcely paralleled in the most barbarous ages, and totally unworthy the Head of a civilized nation.—He has constrained our fellow Citizens taken Captive on the high Seas to bear Arms against their Country, to become the executioners of their friends and Brethren, or to fall themselves by their Hands.—He has excited domestic insurrections amongst us, and has endeavoured to bring on the inhabitants of our frontiers, the merciless Indian Savages, whose known rule of warfare, is an undistinguished destruction of all ages, sexes and conditions. In every stage of these Oppressions We have Petitioned for Redress in the most humble terms: Our repeated Petitions have been answered only by repeated injury. A Prince, whose character is thus marked by every act which may define a Tyrant, is unfit to be the ruler of a free people. Nor have We been wanting in attentions to our British brethren. We have warned them from time to time of attempts by their legislature to extend an unwarrantable jurisdiction over us. We have reminded them of the circumstances of our emigration and settlement here. We have appealed to their native justice and magnanimity, and we have conjured them by the ties of our common kindred to disavow these usurpations, which, would inevitably interrupt our connections and correspondence. They too have been deaf to the voice of justice and of consanguinity. We must, therefore, acquiesce in the necessity, which denounces our Separation, and hold them, as we hold the rest of mankind, Enemies in War, in Peace Friends.—

We, therefore, the Representatives of the united States of America, in General Congress, Assembled, appealing to the Supreme Judge of the world for the rectitude of our intentions, do, in the Name, and by Authority of the good People of these Colonies, solemnly publish and declare, That these United Colonies are, and of Right ought to be Free and Independent States; that they are Absolved from all Allegiance to the British Crown, and that all political connection between them and the State of Great Britain, is and ought to be totally dissolved; and that as Free and Independent States, they have full Power to levy War, conclude Peace, contract Alliances, establish Commerce, and to do all other Acts and Things which Independent States may of right do.—And for the support of this Declaration, with a firm reliance on the protection of divine Providence, we mutually pledge to each other our Lives, our Fortunes and our sacred Honor.

John Hancock

Button Gwinnett
Lyman Hall
Geo Walton.

Wm Hooper
Joseph Hewes,
John Penn

Edward Rutledge.

Thos Heyward Junr.
Thomas Lynch Junr.
Arthur Middleton

Samuel Chase
Wm Paca
Thos Stone
Charles Carroll of Carrollton

George Wythe
Richard Henry Lee
Th Jefferson
Benj Harrison
Thos Nelson jr.
Francis Lightfoot Lee
Carter Braxton

Robt Morris
Benjamin Rush
Benj. Franklin
John Morton
Geo Clymer
Jas. Smith
Geo. Taylor
James Wilson
Geo. Ross
Caesar Rodney
Geo Read
Tho M:Kean

Wm Floyd
Phil. Livingston
Frans Lewis
Lewis Morris
Richd Stockton
Jno Witherspoon
Fras Hopkinson
John Hart
Abra Clark

Josiah Bartlett
Wm Whipple
Saml Adams
John Adams
Robt Treat Paine
Elbridge Gerry
Step Hopkins
William Ellery
Roger Sherman
Sam el Huntington
Wm Williams
Oliver Wolcott
Matthew Thornton

For Huang Luo Yi,
a.k.a. Sullivan Wong Rockwell
—A.R.

For Niko
—F.C.

Grateful acknowledgment to Tameka Bradley Hobbs, PhD, Author and Historian, for providing input on the text.

Carolrhoda Books
A division of Lerner Publishing Group, Inc.
241 First Avenue North
Minneapolis, MN 55401 USA

For reading levels and more information, look up this title at www.lernerbooks.com.

The photos in this book are used with the permission of: National Archives, front end page; Schomburg Center
for Research in Black Culture, Manuscripts, Archives and Rare Books Division, The New York Public Library,
The New York Public Library, Astor, Lenox and Tilden Foundations, back end page, p. 29; © French School, (18th
century)/Musee de la Ville de Paris, Musee Carnavalet, Paris, France/Archives Charmet/Bridgeman Images, p. 32.

Design by Laura Rinne and Danielle Carnito
Main body text set in Aptifer Slab LT Pro Semibold 16/22. Typeface provided by Linotype AG.
The illustrations in this book were created using oil and erasure.

Library of Congress Cataloging-in-Publication Data

Names: Rockwell, Anne F., author. | Cooper, Floyd, illustrator.
Title: A spy called James : the true story of James Lafayette, Revolutionary War double agent / by Anne Rockwell ;
    illustrated by Floyd Cooper.
Description: Minneapolis : Carolrhoda Books, [2015]
Identifiers: LCCN 2014011569 | ISBN 9781467749336 (lib. bdg. : alk. paper) | ISBN 9781467761789 (eb pdf)
Subjects: LCSH: Lafayette, James Armistead, 1760?–1830—Juvenile literature. | United States—History—
    Revolution, 1775–1783—African Americans—Biography—Juvenile literature. | Spies—United States—
    Biography—Juvenile literature.
Classification: LCC E269.N3 R625 2015 | DDC 973.3/85092—dc23

LC record available at http://lccn.loc.gov/2014011569

Manufactured in the United States of America
1-36431-17035-3/4/2016

A Spy Called James

The TRUE STORY of JAMES LAFAYETTE, Revolutionary War DOUBLE AGENT

ANNE ROCKWELL

illustrated by FLOYD COOPER

CAROLRHODA BOOKS
MINNEAPOLIS

ON OCTOBER 19, 1781, the Battle of Yorktown ended with an American victory over British forces. Thanks to the help of French troops, including General Lafayette, the colonists were now poised to win the war they'd been fighting against the British since 1775. With the war's end, America would be a free country.

One of the last things British general Cornwallis did before returning to England was to visit Lafayette's camp. Cornwallis wondered how his army of redcoats had been beaten by the young French general.

The two generals had at least a couple of things in common. Both came from impressive families, and both had impressive names. Cornwallis's full name was Charles Cornwallis, 1st Marquess and 2nd Earl Cornwallis, Viscount Brome, Baron Cornwallis of Eye.

The Frenchman's full name was Marie-Joseph-Paul-Yves-Roch-Gilbert du Motier, Marquis de Lafayette. In France, his friends called him Gilbert. But in America, he was simply Lafayette.

It's easy to imagine that the American Revolution and the fate of the thirteen colonies were in the hands of men like these, men whose names were destined to be famous: Franklin. Jefferson. Washington . . .

After all, not long after the war ended, streets, schools, parks, and cities would be named after these men.

A list of names had also
helped start the war.
Many of these famous men
signed the Declaration
of Independence, telling
King George of England
the colonies would be free.

But America would not have won independence without the courage of thousands of people whose names never became famous.

Cornwallis saw one such man in Lafayette's camp during his visit. He must have known in a flash exactly how Lafayette had defeated him.

The person Cornwallis saw was known by one name. But without him, the war might have ended very differently.

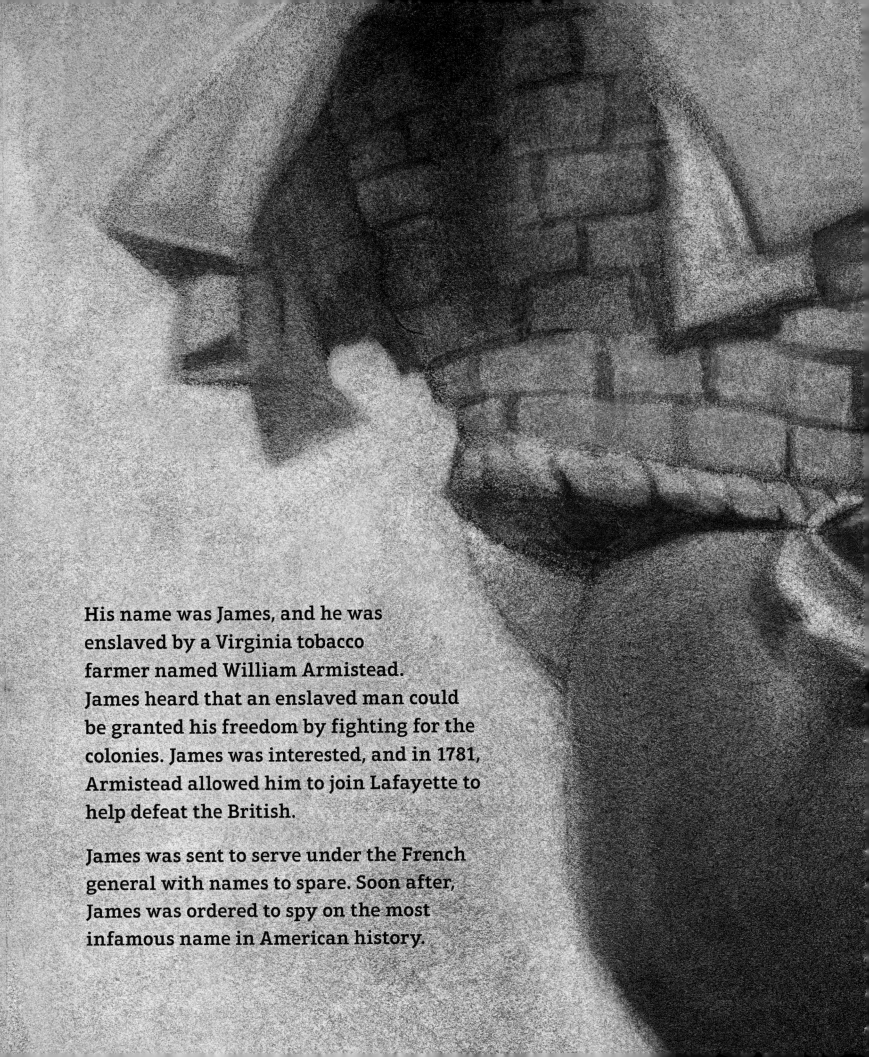

His name was James, and he was enslaved by a Virginia tobacco farmer named William Armistead. James heard that an enslaved man could be granted his freedom by fighting for the colonies. James was interested, and in 1781, Armistead allowed him to join Lafayette to help defeat the British.

James was sent to serve under the French general with names to spare. Soon after, James was ordered to spy on the most infamous name in American history.

Benedict Arnold began the Revolutionary War on the side of the colonists. He fought bravely in many battles. But Arnold did not feel appreciated. After being passed over for promotion in 1779, Arnold secretly switched sides. By the next year, he was spying for the British, working against his own commander, General George Washington.

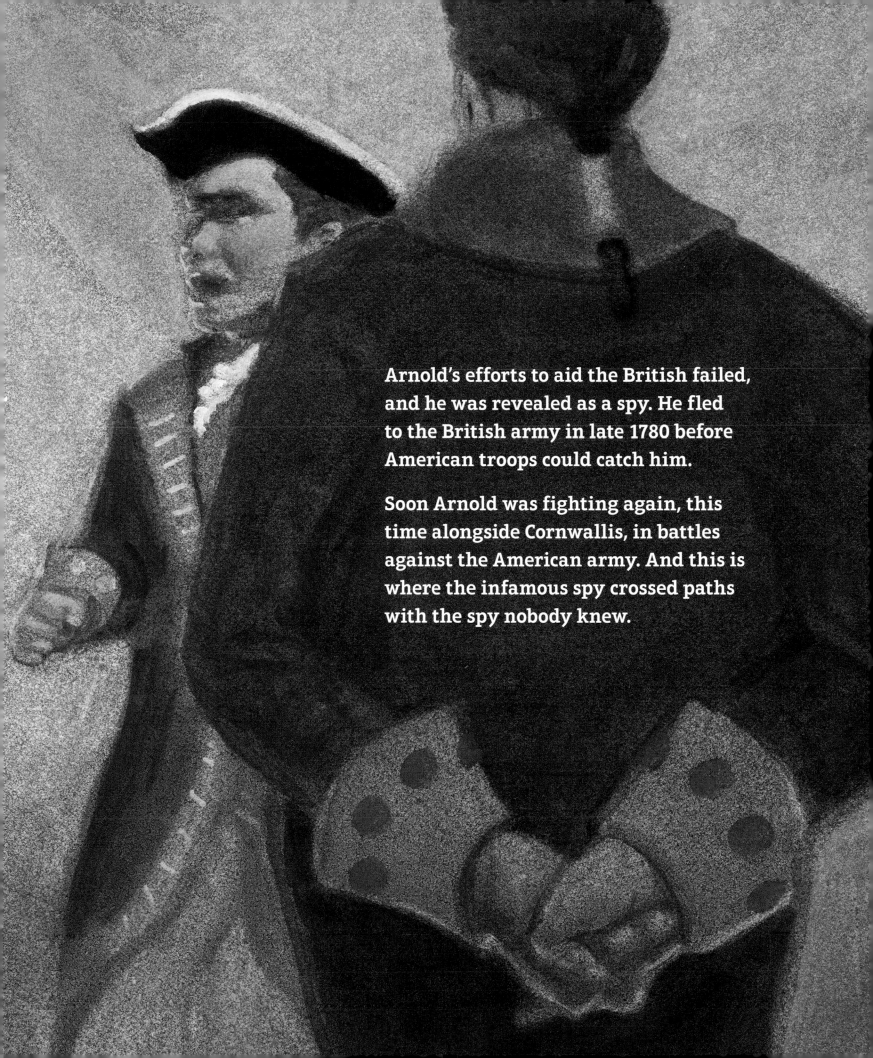

Arnold's efforts to aid the British failed, and he was revealed as a spy. He fled to the British army in late 1780 before American troops could catch him.

Soon Arnold was fighting again, this time alongside Cornwallis, in battles against the American army. And this is where the infamous spy crossed paths with the spy nobody knew.

On orders from Lafayette, James dressed in tatters and presented himself as a runaway slave to Cornwallis and Benedict Arnold. He offered to guide British soldiers along the unfamiliar roads. He foraged for food for the troops. The soldiers accepted his help, but no one paid much attention to him.

This was a big mistake.

Cornwallis, Arnold, and their troops said things in front of James that they shouldn't have. James saw secret plans and maps. And then he snuck away and passed on what he heard to Lafayette.

The British had such faith in James that they asked him to spy on the Americans for them.

James agreed. He carried information to Lafayette from the British and gave the British misleading information about American plans.

Working as a double agent was incredibly risky. If the British discovered James was a spy, they would do what they did to all spies: hang him immediately. And if American soldiers who didn't know who he was caught him carrying papers to the British, they too might execute James as a spy.

But James was never caught. Within a year, the information he passed to Lafayette allowed the colonial army to trap Cornwallis at Yorktown. The British army had no choice but to surrender.

James was in Lafayette's camp when Cornwallis paid his visit. No one knows for sure if James saw the look on Cornwallis's face when the general realized who had fooled him, but it's not hard to imagine James would have felt satisfied.

The war officially ended in 1783 with American victory, but there was no victory for James. While he received credit for his spying during the war, these activities didn't earn James the freedom he expected. Such freedom was reserved for black soldiers in the American army, not spies.

Three years after the fighting ceased, James was still enslaved.

When Lafayette learned about James's circumstances, he was outraged.

He gave James a certificate, written in Lafayette's own hand, declaring he should be free:

This is to certify that the Bearer by the name of James has done Essential Services to me while I had the Honour to Command in this State. His Intelligences from the Enemy's Camp were industriously collected and most faithfully deliver'd. He properly acquitted himself with some important Commissions I gave him and appears to me entitled to every reward his Situation can admit of. Done under my hand, Richmond, November 21st, 1784.

Lafayette

Two years later, the Virginia legislature made James a free man. In tribute to what Lafayette did for him, he took the last name Lafayette.

JAMES LAFAYETTE WAS FINALLY FREE.

AUTHOR'S NOTE

Much about James Lafayette's life is unknown. He was born into slavery in Virginia in about 1748. From his birth until he was freed, James was owned by William Armistead.

During the Revolutionary War (1775–1783), William Armistead sold military supplies to the American army. In the summer of 1781, he and James were in Richmond, Virginia, supplying General Lafayette's troops. But Lafayette needed more than just supplies, so Armistead allowed James to join Lafayette either as a servant or a spy.

In all, historians estimate that about five thousand African Americans fought for the Continental Army. After the war ended in 1783, the state of Virginia emancipated slaves who had enlisted in place of their owners. The Virginia law, however, did not extend to slaves who had served as spies.

At about that time, James began seeking freedom for himself. In December 1784, he first petitioned Virginia's General Assembly to grant him free status, but his request was denied. In November 1786, another petition was presented—this time accompanied by Lafayette's letter praising James for his assistance during the war. The General Assembly approved this second petition, officially freeing James on January 9, 1787.

The bill freeing James had a benefit for William Armistead as well: the state of Virginia paid Armistead £250 to compensate him for the loss of his "valuable workman." Presumably Armistead could use these funds to purchase another slave. So while James was finally free, the institution of slavery continued.

This painting by Jean-Baptiste Le Paon, titled *Lafayette at Yorktown*, includes James holding the general's horse. Le Paon was a French artist who created this work between 1783 and 1785.

James Lafayette never wrote about his life, but government documents and tax records provide clues about what he did after he was freed. By 1816, he was married and had at least one son. In that year, James purchased forty acres of farmland near the estate of his former master. Property tax records showed that during his life as a free man, he owned from one to four slaves. In this era, a free black man owning slaves was not unusual.

By the early 1800s, states began paying pensions to soldiers who had served in the Revolutionary War. Because James had not been a soldier, he was not eligible for such payments. So in 1818, he once again petitioned the General Assembly. He was seventy years old, and he stated that he was no longer able to make a living as a laborer. The petition was approved, and James was given sixty dollars immediately and forty dollars per year for the rest of his life.

James and Lafayette met one last time when Lafayette returned to the United States in 1824. During a celebration at Yorktown, a large crowd, including James, greeted the Frenchman. Lafayette saw James, called to him by name, and the two men embraced.

James spent his remaining years on his farm in New Kent County, and he died there on August 9, 1830, at the age of eighty-two. By that time, slavery had been abolished in some northern states, but all enslaved African Americans did not achieve freedom until June 19, 1865, after the end of the Civil War.

Research note: No other books about James exist, although he is mentioned in a number of books about Revolutionary War heroes and African American heroes. A particularly helpful source in telling James's story was John Salmon's article, "'A Mission of the Most Secret and Important Kind': James Lafayette and American Espionage in 1781," published in the Autumn 1981 issue of Virginia Calvacade. *Various sources refer to James as either James Lafayette or James Armistead Lafayette after he was freed. While he has become popularly known by the latter name, the historical record does not show that he ever officially adopted the surname of his master, William Armistead.*

FURTHER READING

Grady, Cynthia. *Like a Bird: The Art of the American Slave Song*. Minneapolis: Millbrook Press, 2016. This picture book presents thirteen spirituals, accompanied by paintings depicting the experiences of slaves and free African Americans, including James Lafayette.

Johnson, Angela. *All Different Now: Juneteenth, the First Day of Freedom*. New York: Simon & Schuster Books for Young Readers, 2014. Told from the point of view of a young enslaved girl, this picture book recounts the story of the first Juneteenth, the day the last of the slaves in the South were freed.

Nelson, Kadir. *Heart and Soul: The Story of America and African Americans*. New York: Balzer + Bray, 2011. This distinctive illustrated book introduces readers to the history of African Americans in the United States.

Sanders, Nancy I. *America's Black Founders: Revolutionary Heroes & Early Leaders; with 21 Activities*. Chicago: Chicago Review Press, 2010. Read about a range of African Americans who helped the United States gain independence. This book also includes recipes for colonial foods as well as other activities.

Woelfle, Gretchen. *Mumbet's Declaration of Independence*. Minneapolis: Carolrhoda Books, 2014. Discover the little-known story of an African American slave in Massachusetts who successfully went to court in 1781 to win freedom for herself and her daughter.

This is to Certify that the Bearer by the Name of James
Has done Essential Services to me While I Had the Honour to
Command in this State. His Intelligence from the Enemy's
Camp were Industriously Collected and More faithfully Delivered
He perfectly Acquitted Himself with Some Important Commissions
I gave him and Appears to me Entitled to Every Reward his
Situation Can Admit of. Done Under My Hand. Richmond
November 21st 1784.
Lafayette